When Correlation is Causation

and other poems

Heikki Huotari

Better Than Starbucks
Publications

When Correlation is Causation

Copyright © 2021 by Heikki Huotari

All rights reserved. This book or any portion thereof may not be reproduced or used in any manner whatsoever without the express written permission of author and the publisher except for the use of brief quotations in a book review or scholarly journal.

First Printing: ISBN 978-1-7376219-3-5

Cover Image: Yellow Circle by László Moholy-Nagy

Better Than Starbucks Publications
P.O.Box 673, Mayo, FL 32066

for my mother

Table of Contents

Concurrent Birdsong

When Correlation Is Causation	11
Parentheses Etcetera	12
Let My Great Apes Go	13
This Vista	14
What An Amoeba	15
Peach	16
Lucid	17
How The Leopard Got Its Stripes	18
Portmanteau	19
Snood 2	20
Fixed Position	21
A Bountiful Supply	22
XOR	23
Wishes Whispered Once	24
Overlapping Umbra	25
On My Return To Jupiter	26
The Ingredients Are Secret	27
Aubade	28
Bimodal	29

Freedom Wheel

Geocentric	33
With Sisyphus	34
How The Eldorado Got Its Tailfins	35
Center Of Mass 2	36
Defined By Broken Bones	37
Retrospective Proprioception	38
On Athletes Needs	39
Presocratic	40

Beeline	41
Flood Plain	42
On Empty	43
As Transparent as It Gets	44
Sousaphone	45
The Amoeba and The Paramecium	46
Semi Autonomic	47
For Finite Crime	48
That Palm Tree Is a Cell Phone Tower	49
In Dog Years	50
Pigs In Pokes	51

Among Homunculi

One Per Waterfall	55
Gratuitous Ode	56
Simulacrum, 1969	57
Acceptance	58
Right Align	59
Reciprocal	60
Piano Drop	61
The Garden of Earthly Delights	62
The Law of Large Numbers	63
When Gravitons Amass	64
Stringing Clouds Along	65
Quid Pro Quo	66
Woke From Coma Speaking French	67
After Fact	68
Two Science Daily Spin-offs	69
As Of	70
Return to Sturgis	71
Who's On First	72
The Lucky Customer	73

Remote Sensing

Optics	77
Syllogism 5	78
In Which I Kick the Tires	79
It's The Thought That Counts	80
Free The Aegis!	81
Hook And Eye	82
Photon	83
Mechanical Advantage	84
Ex Falso Quodlibet	85
The Contact Sport	86
Watercolor	87
Expected Value	88
On Stalking the Apostle Paul	90

Scenic Overlook

Sleep Start	93
Scenic Overlook 1	94
Scenic Overlook 2	95
Scenic Overlook 3	96
Scenic Overlook 4	97
Scenic Overlook 5	98
Scenic Overlook 6	99
Scenic Overlook 7	100
Scenic Overlook 8	102

Citations	103
About the Author	105

Concurrent Birdsong

When Correlation Is Causation

To the horseless carriage I say get a horse. The naked eye sees two of everything but averages the brace of quail. Dear Liza, in this galaxy there's no black hole, dear Liza, with what should I fix it? As distracted, these contributors are mere participants. Their honorifics migrate night and day. They're oppositely gendered of their own volition. Innocently and or legally, their names have changed. One twin surrounds another in a glut of love. As my convergence is conditional, to sum to any number I'll be reconfigured. Stake your claim; I'll cry for me and mine. As fear is focused barely satiated taste buds blossom and as sunburn and consumption of ice cream are correlated correlation is causation.

Parentheses Etcetera

First cause then last effect. How well will houses balance on an earth that isn't there? I felt an urge to sculpt with plastic pipe and canvas likenesses of likenesses. A thing with feathers perching in the soul is worth two things with feathers rehabilitated incompletely. As the tombstone topples and the accolade is face down, reconsider twice white lies and double negatives and please excuse my dear aunt Sally past abstraction, as from my ear to God's lips this walking metaphor is less a Bahnhofstrasse than a sand trap.

Let My Great Apes Go

Casual or causal be the rap, but be an interval without endpoints, a sea of slot machine with gratitude, resentment and points in between. A patriot is sounding one alarm if two are walking by and two if three are loitering. It's 10 AM. Your music splits no ear. The path of least resistance far from fixed, what this continuum is missing is concurrent birdsong. Typhoid Mary, mother of the super-spreader, mathematical induction, who's on n plus first?

This Vista

Circumventing user-friendliness we're spelling out the ats and dots. Sandpipers effortlessly find the contour line. What need have we of grace? This helicopter has a heart. Embedded metals of an expectation juggle three beliefs. These dreams keep meat from bones. In anterooms the shoes remove. Cylindrical, so by its base my airspace is defined, by basic human rights. Commuters, first responders, were abiding safely in the suburbs. Lo, no angel, said unto them, Would you tune to news?

What An Amoeba

In a county where the prison is the one employer, fresh from reverie I'm playing no piano with four hands. The most efficient means of moving mass so far, I hereby donate my pineal gland to social science. Siri recommends a lane change and becomes increasingly insistent so I say to Siri, Siri, we are not alone. The ear behind which my come-hither flower is installed decided by a coin toss, thou shalt take no other name in vain. Looking over my left shoulder I'll be walking backwards, using what were stabilizing muscles for propulsion. Pareidolia finds favor in God's eyes. My vertigo is idiot-proof. What a coroner I am, what an amoeba — as my corner has three hats I'm going anaerobic slowly.

Peach

The serenade is suitable. On hearing car alarms I care. Your calling sunrise peach won't disallow my doing so. The fountain pen of age is leaking into my shirt pocket. Spontaneity, is that what you'll be wearing to the sacrifice? The serenade is suitable. On hearing car alarms I care. No Loch Ness Monster gets in my way. Armchair executioner, what inadvertent innocence will you be weaponizing now? If thy glass eye delight thee pop it in. A broken biorhythm is correct once every other day. The serenade is suitable. On hearing car alarms I care.

Lucid

If they were ashes they were snowflakes and they might have melted on some tongue so what about the difference between vertical and horizontal don't they understand? As in the trail of bread crumbs there's a fork, a joke, two stories of an origin, if poor or poor but honest twins are switched with twins at birth event horizons dilate like an iris and subtended angles of invisibility like opportunities abound. To see if you're asleep try turning on and off the light, to see if you're a hero too.

How The Leopard Got Its Stripes

As fearing loss of love was all the rage we might have practiced at compassion. Please come with me to my senses. As redeemers role-reverse and sin intuitively I stop dying twice a day. An aggregate of witnesses positioned at an intersection recommend that surrogates be cloned, that clones be single ply, that flying pies collide. A sum of chasms is a vacuum.

Portmanteau

To the naked man and woman God said, Who said you have one iota of redeeming social value? Bounded by tautology and contradiction, fun was had by all but twenty. If you crossed a picket line which was invisible then the ekphrasis that you sang was seething. Islands of potential energy, the gods are bumping fists. Five sheets of cardboard on the concrete and you still can't sleep? Don't pay attention to that pervert, Rorschach — symmetry is where you find it. Keep your eye on that expected value, Esperanza — sum the products of the outcomes and their probabilities. You're just the messenger and when the rapture happens you'll be busy training your replacement.

Snood 2

I'm not the kind of flightless bird that turns lights on and off for no good reason. There are more criteria than I can shake a stick at. Weighing options is a prelude to abstention. I, a lamp, might go out empty handed too. Your hairnet keeps your hair out of my food. I see endangered species and my mechanism's ecumenical. Big spenders of belief rely on floating Moses. Moses, you were not the clone of me — whenever we were nominally radially in agreement we were diametrically opposed. I will have that inclusive aura. Microscopic arms and legs on platelets take me home.

The Fixed Position

You don't care about it but you think I ought to. Alternating mirror neurons, some like sea legs, I can see, like sequins and, as gravity is stipulated and a paper of no pins granted me, I flee to sleep. Who gives this body not to be the playground of a workaround? Considering the hands of Meltdown Man directing traffic, toes in tulips and their noses, so bereft of essence I move molecules the color of a keep. Consideration but in spinning lily and emotion but in educated flea, the may fly's love life is the may fly's life. Vicinity imprisons me and sets you free.

A Bountiful Supply

When in venery you wash your hands of others' hands and when in laughter's afternoon, a random sample qua committee of white men, as white as if they've seen a ghost, is chosen. They're a people. They're a people and a bubble. They're a people and a bubble and a puddle and the triplets and the twins who witness this don't disagree. There is a dotted line then blinding light then short-term gain. From ends of life too close to call you strew rose petals so the hand that feeds you is food too.

XOR

Hell's spells are broken here, the highest and the lowest scores ignored. One butterfly to reward bad behavior and to reconstrue good deeds, one question to put coins in my tin cup, I'll be adjacent and I'll be abject. The sharpest tools in watersheds extend to electricity then logic. Mentalists' opinions past exaggeration, models are most accurate far from extremes. Abiding in the valley of no shadow or no sunlit field, luxuriating in no plethora or squirming in no dearth, behold the XOR gate.*

* An XOR gate is an electric circuit corresponding to the exclusive or.

Wishes Whispered Once

Though I thumb through to overlays of shadows I don't go off script. As Heisenberg "The Principal" is unimaginable, so pro forma is my promenade, not problematic — my ad hoc committee with authority to enforce is equipped. I am a stand-aside comedian and under no duress so take me seriously folks and throw me tokens of appreciation. Photo IDs hanging from their pork-pie hats, discriminating zealots comfort me to what extent they're able so I ask, Will this be on the test of time?

Overlapping Umbra

My head of hair is either beauty, brain or brawn, the modicum of spirit that lives on. The gods are ugly, weak or stupid when they walk like white men on their heels, their heel prints deep in snow. The Santa Claus to end all Santa Clauses is the anti Santa Claus. It's turn-about but not fair play — these corners are belied by spiders and apprentices and kinds of symmetry that shoes are prone to — club foot, pigeon toes. An atmosphere, a rabbit's hat, as maximal for two as minimal for three, if I were you I would be me and not just juxtapose.

On My Return to Jupiter

On the circle of convergence nothing's guaranteed. A power series may converge or not. On an eventual horizon if that mass is critical of me I may not take it well. Take over gravity. Right circular the cylinder that has one floor, one ceiling and one wall. Describe the daisy chain but don't explain it. In the plane two rigid motions are rotation and translation. How about that other opposite of me, the one that's coming at me through the rye? That cat was not or was confined to Schrodinger's gas chamber as that cat did not or did commit that heinous crime. So render unto Lola that which Lola wants. Good news: good news is nigh.

The Ingredients Are Secret

To predators I'm shocking or I'm toxic, just one taste of me completes a circuit or induces an hallucination. At what occupancy I break even is proprietary. When I'm on a pedestal or precipice some pseudo-random actor serenades me with five sizes of guitar. There is no pareidolia in this backwater but us direct objects. Call it the eleventh hour. The existence of soft tissue is a given, bridges burn and portals misconstrue. The water table's tilted or our roots have different depths or we are ushers or have flashlights or we're instigating riots. I'm like, Would you like an epicycle with that astrophysics, Ptolemy? and Ptolemy's like, Don't mind if I do.

Aubade

Takeover be not hostile and makeup take up no arms. If Schrodinger and Heisenberg go fishing, walk into a bar or both, who lapses last? And if you're grieving then you're grieving in a house of mirrors; if you're dancing then you're dancing on some grave. You pay the fine in pennies. May the pennies make a statement. Peter Pan effect and state collapse a classical equivalence, you'll be a moiety and not conjoin. You'll have a year's supply of passion and the axes on which your concentric spheres will spin will be orthogonal. By bioluminescing, almost-doctors of philosophy will see you now.

Bimodal

There are exactly two desserts and neither's just. A chain's a causal chain or not. The gamblers are or are not welcome. Bells and whistles equally repelling and attracting, woe to those whose casual mutations are incorporated into selfish genes. Until I hear a minor triad from a baby grand piano I can't sleep. As some heads are synecdoches in lieu of hands on deck, to what avail, to what extent am I mistaken? If there were not something there why would they try to hide it? Alternately, if you can't afford it then you have to ask.

Freedom Wheel

Geocentric

Reality the best in me, TV, the living tissue, would repair itself. Diversity meant some were even whiter. With a mirror and a laser my propinquity was ever measured to within a millimeter. Holidays, in lieu of being beaten, I would balance on my knee a soggy paper plate, take rage in grapes and waves. As singular the scissor, so six-sided was the die. It's my head that the joke goes over. I'm the one on whom the irony is lost.

With Sisyphus

I treat my treadmill like a gerbil treats its freedom wheel. I'm conscientiously objecting. When centripetal, some mechanisms are not atavisms and some mechanisms freely reproduce. In present Texas, love and marriage go together like a horseless carriage and a car without a driver. What's the endgame? Where's the harm? I'm not an actor but I doctor one. That's Doctor of Gratuitous Philosophy to you. As of some twenty umbras no square circle is invented, none are spoken either of or for.

How The Eldorado Got Its Tailfins

Ostensibly reed instruments are instruments that I read into. Saxophones are, like most plumb bobs, out of true. I wake up knowing where you are but not where I am. Opposites are not attracting or my fast-food order is to go or I must bide. I'm no comedian, try as I might. The job is clean so no one has to do it. One lorn horse is torn between two hostelries but is it equilibrium? Are those the evidences of the senses? Are those eyes like lights or are those lights like eyes?

Center Of Mass 2

The halves of coconuts to simulate the passing canter of aloofness and synecdoche to no known mental block, the misremembered word is either *ambush* or *allotment.* As I have but one side, one good side, my adolescence uncontested, halfway through my run of luck I think therefore I exit, I may be a crackpot or the personality you see tomorrow on TV. I take no umbrage. Underdamped, my mass in perpetuity is oscillating independently and to the coefficient of velocity it thumbs its nose. Nor suffering assumption nor when light makes right I'm simultaneous and simultaneously I arrive, no disincentive and no centipede, my faces regular, triangular, hexagonal, my applicant's credentials decorated and illuminated and in rows.

Defined By Broken Bones

I say I'll have happiness and if not happiness then liberty and if not liberty then life, and my horizon rises like one eyebrow. In the catalog of catalogs I circle certain words. A sculptor, I remove from plethora what is not dearth. I'm dancing on the water table, having slaked no thirst. A rose between my teeth, I'm sounding my alignment. If you won't be in the business of refinement may I bring my own Greek chorus? May I bring my own refrain?

Retrospective Proprioception

Highs and lows truncated, media are speaking off the record to the scattered facets that their minds are on. The minimum is minus rumble, rubble, bubble. French is senseless and the royal oui an iterate, amused, symmetric to a fault. The systems in the basement and subbasement are respectively mechanical and mad. Misleading syllabi are swinging from no chandelier. Blessed be professionals, their pensions vested, rising right to left. Call them instructions if you care or dare to. In an urn remains are blooming as inclusively as the aloha says the oboe is exotic too.

On Athletes' Needs

My tincture so diluted it might not contain a single subatomic particle, I jump from joy and have no hair to tear. How mathematical the expectation leveraging the random person, place or thing, the thing that is abiding in the field! The elegant solution is the quality of mercy and homogeneous. Enabling the saint, whatever is most relegated to the microscopic detail has or tells the future, overrides, smooth-shod, the past. On stilts, my building barely bulges but contains a multitude of me. My nylon stockings making shushing noises of my thighs, the present tenses. Add identifiers to them, they will curse you later but it's good fun now. It's what an athlete needs a ton of.

Presocratic

A submarine, I learn from rabid activists what not to promise. Those who are not children should be heard not seen. When wooing two, the oxeye daisy's petals fall in multiples of four: love-love, love-not, not-love, not-not. The broken heart, a working clock, is in alignment twice.

The first half-hour of altered consciousness is free, the engineer who doesn't know what sin is drops the first piano and the word-for-word translation from the language of love is sufficient. Paradigms will incompletely shift, both old and new gods have a hand in. We will not be welcomed so enthusiastically again.

Which voice goes with which body? On the verge of perfect, balanced on the not-a-step, I see another ladder. In the vortex where the rapture happens faster, Lazarus can answer Jesus, Jesus, *You* come *in*.

Beeline

Gratuitous philosophy, philosophy for two — my tourist is as territorial as you, a thoughtful penny on a rail is coinciding, and a name next to a random rose will sell as well as roses do. My heart was plagiarizing up to now so to my dying disyllabic heart beat I would kick and I would turn and I would improvise until the better understanding would be had of all of Idaho. These implications come in pairs of pears. The peach slice slithers back into the can. What instrument of torture's unsupported? As some synesthetes put pigs on lipstick, wish and whisper, so the crow.

Flood Plain

First full-moon morning of the year. When, arm in arm, three women span the path, I step aside to let them pass and one says, Sorry, we're on owl watch. As the self-serve copier is jammed, the self has fled the scene. From my life story my life story is expunged. The spectrum's endpoints now tautology and contradiction, following a night of flying I put on my rain and raiment one palm up and one elbowed appendage at a time.

On Empty

I'm underwriting disappearing ink with innocence and vice versa — I'm more Honest Abe than Honest Abe. The hearts of artichokes beguiling me, my strings go zing. The deck is stacked, Cassandra leaves them laughing, pugilists are languishing in rope and canvas corners then, inflatable but not inflated, Santa's in a plastic puddle, as are reindeer, as in Phoenix Arizona it's another shirt-sleeve Christmas Eve.

As Transparent as It Gets

Just because you're parasailing doesn't mean this call's not coming from inside your house. As mirror neurons turn, I'm casting demons and fly fishing with them. In each multi-facet is a hidden hook. It's possible that Satan is deceiving me. With Gertrude Stein I beg to differ then along with Gertrude Stein I beg to differ. What is not yet yellow is a yellow cat. What will they think of next? A palace for each personage and vice versa. Veni, vici, vidi, says restroom graffiti and, The joke is in your hand why are you looking here? Nor filler nor refrain, this content will not stop but is it pheasant under glass?

Sousaphone

When kindness has no clothing there's no end of faces, edges, vertices and instruments in aggregate, their noses flat against the glass. In adumbration of felicity, a measurable subset of a measurable space is an event delineated by an endless monologue. So what can knowledgeable great apes do but write and writhe? Debriefing, I'm the midpoint of an interval whose radius is less than one, and having traveled singly to this gleaming operating theater, I'm reaching for my seat belt. Nowhere near a vacuum or a chasm, I could be a feather or a bowling ball. In consequence, beloved equally of hearts and minds, my double negative is strong and silent twice.

The Amoeba and The Paramecium

The time not right, competing species had their roles reversed to only two avails, the credit's and demerit's mutual annihilation. Can't lie down with dogs and can't get up with fleas. The body not of water, not of knowledge and the perfect body not of ashes, not of dust, concomitant of opposites, the call's not coming from without — a rising tide lifts each of Noah's boats. Dishonor mimics to whatever extent they deserve. Did I say to dishonor mimics? I meant, mimic all dis-honorees. For it is mauve and puce to do so so to do. The empty sleeve rotated three degrees is good as new.

Semi Autonomic

My moiety is yours. I would endorse a contact sport if you would and together we could take one for the team. My military clock is right nine times, nine oxymorons in a row. And Jesus washed his elbows and his eyebrows and each hand that didn't wash itself. What hug did not some bear at some point offer, and what checkerboard, so red and black, so like a painted cattle guard, to me.

For Finite Crime

A crescent moon, a crosscut saw and how. If to each raindrop some particulate adheres then why not iron a wrinkle in? If in the intersection of two bags of bones one false alarm is traded for another, then my heart is not a sponge, then for each two pianos there are seven hands, a candelabra falling and the property for whom the property is horizontally divided. Rather than a metaphor, I'd have a metaphor with teeth. What outer space needs now is rage, blind rage, so says the man who was an island, vehement, then, sizzling, succumbed.

That Palm Tree Is a Cell Phone Tower

Programs running in my background have minds of their own. A school of, by and for some fish, I need truckloads of irony to ward off random facts. If loitering were once illegal, now it is an idée fixe, so fabricate me while you have the chops. Parametrized by arc length, I anticipate no hairpin turn. Outside of time it's dark, too dark to read, and no one screens my calls. Another active-shooter drill, another true-to-life alarm, the broken body clock, a customer, is always right. My immune system turns on me, a chosen people once I light up like a town. So what diphthong is she exaggerating in my absence, what sunspot is she adopting now?

In Dog Years

The dog says, I'll have what the cats are having. Arbiters of taste are suiting up to go outside and be extended. The intruder washing dishes knows no oath. The chairs are chained and glisten — give their grievances some air! If in a hoop of hoops I would have independent axes of rotation, I would work the room and play a tiny violin. Without a cautery the nerve would never end but fray. If snowflakes played the odds would they amass like random samples or be self-sufficient? Those who choose to live in vales of tears need not complain.

Pigs In Pokes
yet in my flesh shall I see God —Job 19:26

The fig leaf of imagination advertises unknown content. Moonlight is the best infection — look for parallelograms of sunlight any day. The language I'll be speaking is a function of what bed I slept in last, and on which side. The non-stop-talking probabilities are within intervals of confidence, the horseless carriages are superseded by the driverless, the universe that's at eye level is the universe the universe is recommending and in this, my lifetime, antipodes will be ice-free.

Among Homunculi

One Per Waterfall

Guy walks by an isobar and lightning goes on strike. Translucence and viscosity are keen to please. As pulling is more natural than pushing you may travel back in time lit from within so if it's structure that you want consider this conditional. Presuming they'll exaggerate, if I were you among homunculi I'd keep it clean. Nobody knows how artificially intelligent you really are. Your vital sign is not an island and the rope you're at the end of either fortunately or unfortunately isn't yours.

Gratuitous Ode

My only comfort is my circular paraboloid is finally with the satellites. My nights unnumbered, many lilies of the field and Tinker Bell still need continuous attention so as not to spin out of control. Your footfall, your false start opaque, your hot-house blossom is gigantic, not just redolent of rotting flesh. The big bang's fifty-two-card pickup is in progress; your goodbye is why. What rhyme or reason did you think I'd fail to interdict?

Simulacrum, 1969

To founder or to flounder not to founder is to scale fate up or swim in saline. Scenic overlook elided, polka dots of center-pivot irrigation systems are not possible or are not green. If I have seven words for "argumentum ad absurdum" but not one for "avatar" then Carol and Louise and I agree it's fine to walk and halfway through an incandescent intersection leave the borrowed car.

Acceptance

As this time space is variously viscous, this effect precedes this cause. This water walks on what this water walks on. It's an anti-miracle: there's nothing in this jar. The cricket is a given. Red and blue wheelbarrows clutter up the one dimension that I haven't used. They're prone to motion, have potential as pedestrians and once per revolution I look on in awe. The gaze that I avert is physical not mental. With no physical phenomenon am I at war.

Right Align

All hands and hooks for hands on deck, there is no zombie to whom I can't kowtow. Denizens and penitents can smell malfeasance from a mile. From parallel to perpendicular, so in a row three group psychoses. Neither virtuoso be nor bad example, one with thumbs. The octopus' spirit's willing but the octopus' flesh is weak. As in the vector field a cowlick, at the antipode another. Two of many, one of some, much less an end, I'm rowing, rowing home.

Reciprocal

Random is the enemy of pseudorandom, skinny as a scarecrow. Neurological malfeasance is the order of the day, the aura and the ambiance at odds. The winning probability is in the cast of glances. Virtuoso, shall I see you to your clothing? Blessed are the stopped and frisked for they shall finally know their rights. They shall design an algorithm, then an enterprise, that involves ultraviolets and megabytes. What I feel for Pinocchio Pinocchio can not but feel for me.

Piano Drop

Negation of negations, says the pragmatist. There's no extrapolation but in cutting to the chase, the vaulting pole is broken and, by hovering, the center of mass is maintained. The first half-hour of alternating consciousness is free, the engineer who doesn't know what sin is drops the first piano and the word-for-word translation from the language of love is sufficient. So as not to pick the pace up I'll stay one half step behind. Ten billion years from now, the alien intelligence will miss no episode of I Love Lucy.

The Garden of Earthly Delights

Perpendicular to ecstasy, beribboned entertainers suffer, then control groups, not just fish in barrels, calculate their gradients. Accordingly reoriented, they take baby steps. My private eye is satisfied. As latitude and longitude are woven slowly so some animal might happen by that I can use. Gestalt psychologists are grunting in their jungles, snapping at a password. There's no paper bag that I can't fight my way out of and unsolicited deliveries are mine to do with as I choose.

The Law of Large Numbers

When the blade theatrically retracts into the handle, when they learn to hope like humans all but one will win a consolation prize. It's not so much that we are asymmetric as our symmetry is stayed. My expectations normally distributed with ever smaller standard deviations, I may wonder who you think you're fooling now. As each exigency pleads guilty, ups the ante, you were there so you can't know what happened here so welcome home.

When Gravitons Amass

My faux pas not of fashion but of attitude, my without-form-and-void is handed from one motion-activated nightlight to another. Now my spine is in alignment. Now my lips are sealed. How ellipsoidal, but for their extremities, the chickens, how electrical their circuits. Natural Processes, I'll be the gentle breeze you asked for and the skipping heartbeat. As a boy scout my reward is doubled when I help across the street the soul that has no wish to go. As lie detectors vie for my approval, linear regression is a work in progress then potential energy is edging on kinetic, weather wears redundancy away and gravitons amass.

Stringing Clouds Along

As spurred and hobbled by rubato or diverted by a wobble in its magnetism, north's not true. As gravity depletes my microscopic entourage and softly, shy of dancing, I say yes to every valid syllogism, I say no to that exploding dye pack, that ill-gotten gain. Because all poetry is local, this clandestine meeting never was.

Quid Pro Quo

> *Please please me, oh yeah,
> like I please you.* —The Beatles

Any destination you can question I can question better. Viscerally counterposing relative velocity, you, letter, and, you, spirit are but adjuncts. If some formless furniture increases, some diminishes degrees of freedom and an ordinary object in the painting lays the scale. Undaunted, I would relegate to romance that I'm often talking. When God tells me what to write I write the opposite. If to air grievances is superhuman, then to recommend green eggs and ham is. In your absence matadors are metaphors and taking liberties and talking trash. The glasses of the astronauts are flat, reflective. May the astronauts be nascent swans. What will there be a flying island of when entropy is outlawed? Marching in a molecule, an atom needs no reconstrual.

Woke From Coma Speaking French

When the a priori contradicts itself then anything is possible so what it's all about is either Alfie or the Hokey Pokey and the talking octopus says, *Rough the suspect up,* but later we find out the talking octopus was only joking. Now the talking octopus says, *Where's your sense of humor?* Consequently, you see your asymmetry is in remission as you don't remember which side it was on. The hands of Canada take comfort out of context. Guess who's Doppler shifting now.

After Fact

Beware or not, it's not so much a track as grassy right of way. If you don't know how cold it is you're no comedian and "so cold" doesn't cut it. If you can't take chemistry and physics with you but there's ample room for obligation then that shadow's as distinct from you as if you, pink flamingo, had no leg to stand on. Wake up with mixed feelings and you'll serve sequentially three beatific lives; in ten-dimensional Venn diagrams you'll ascertain as many frequencies as amplitudes. You'll verify my miracle. I'll validate your claim.

Two Science Daily Spin-offs

Transparent and reflective objects are the things of robots' nightmares. As a crow you're quoted out of context. It's no contest: heads I win and tails you lose. The metaphor, when stretched, obeys Hooke's Law and here in spite of grace am I, the silhouette's bright side. As one lung lobe wants oxygen and one wants nitrogen, what is the owner of a lung of lobes to do? I'll be your instantaneous velocity not running average. This abyss was made for me not me and you.

It's in my wiring. I remember doll and pond more readily than couch and cloud. Dismissal is orthogonal to bug *and* feature. Each trichotomy I'll try but once. An owl in outer space, I can't have dry ice cream and eat it and that attitude's no attitude of mine. No billboard says if you will bury me I'll freely lead you to temptation, let you in on my opinion and when numbered, as an onion, be repealed.

As Of

As of one tiny car some clowns climb out and run around and juggle, in one scheme of things three left turns make a right. So I don't question chemistry, in case of loss of contact with reality I'll break the glass. The glass is there for that. To be imagined last, as twisted a resistor as can be, the force of gravity is with me. To a Martian, to a man, all those are patted on the back who do not deign to doubt. I'm raising only eyebrows and there are extenuating circumstances not yet known. To omit outliers and recompute expected values, I'll immerse myself in the Hetch Hetchy Reservoir when the Hetch Hetchy Reservoir is piped to me. The applicable case is Almonds and Alfalfa versus Central Valley Aquifer. The point with no extension endlessly is tipping, there are velvet ropes on stainless posts and everybody has a crux to bear.

Return To Sturgis

If either mime is stymied or one hummingbird says to another, entropy or entropy in ashes, my position and velocity are yours, replacing the already failing muffler by a worse one, beds like statements may be made. This wall will open only on an earthquake, not elliptical, not hyperbolic, and the atmosphere's in oblate fade. A silhouette on my horizon, I belie the laws of logic. As my cause is just and mere so I inherit all that's left. The bobblehead says, *I will be the constant of no ordinary spring.* The alphabet of entropy is tidy as she flies. The book may judge the cover in no fit of extradition. Gravitons are separating and on black and white tiles I make my binary way.

Who's On First

If birds do it, both sides do it. One by one the powers that be collapse. God loves me and God loves me not. If Daisy will not have me, I will be the driver and ride shotgun. Suitable for framing, I will fold the pleasure map. Both hands are minute hands, each hand all thumbs. The fire is out, the water bucket emptied and the steering wheel detached. My other avatar is in the shop.

The Lucky Customer

The bearer of this disquisition is entitled to one out-of-body shopping spree. The autopilot's solipsist is clearly cloned. The bearer's shirt says, I'm With Stupid, and the bearer's sandwich sign is finite. One electric eye winks. Nature's hurdles are surrounded. Now who calls me half disabled favors me — it could have gone bad conduct or dishonorable. Happy birthday Mr Precedent, the aftermath is yours. To metaphysical collateral, obeisances are paid. A scalar matrix wields a wing. Were it not so, I might have colored with the crayons that I had. My eyes dilated, I might not have seen one allopath without a soul. On what occasion and on what horizon does the moon not slowly roll?

Remote Sensing

Optics

Though it's retroactive Christmas pugilism here it's generosity in other places so forgive the substitute stepfather as he knows not what to dream, as canine is to feline as pie is to cake, as one's created in God's image, one's created in God's image in reverse, a purse of cursive pitches, suffering, safari and so far so good. I'm within spitting distance of an ethos and can prove it. May the molecules amend the motions of their molecules, their forces intricately prodigal or simply squandered, almost nominated twice. When etching rectangles on simulated surfaces, they read the wrong directions or the right ones wrongly. Blessed are the wrestlers for they take no shortcuts, ask no favors and foresee no need to reason.

Syllogism 5

Collectibles would be collectible til every human had one. Carpenter's and burglar's tools would be distinguished by intent, to wit, the time of day, the color of the perpetrator's clothes. I would have been a Buddhist but for conscious sweeping or have had an ID on a lanyard in a plastic sleeve. As I invented many clarinets and almost won the Nobel Peace Prize twice, the opposite of fun and profit would include both fun and loss. Anticipating double dealing I would have a graceful segue ready, cartilage and sinew too. To predators, I'm shocking or I'm toxic — just one taste of me completes a circuit or induces an hallucination. An hallucination, one Samaritan invalidates another, saying, My vote cancels yours.

In Which I Kick the Tires

The data were so unequivocal I didn't think to ask, How unequivocal were they? I had both paths parameterized and cataclysms happened only in my absence. Now warts may be wings. The brevity humanity, the summer storm the shadow and the dragonfly, the murder weapon but an icicle and fingerprints and thermal mass. The icicle is not your enemy. The icicle is independent: one's a donor; one's anonymous. They're flying off the shelves as items, as the other items simultaneously are enumerated, denigrated and possessed. My lines of sight are intersecting at a point of order, Mr. Speaker, as in magnifying glasses seconded emotions are not tabled. Zero is no absolute. My eyes are on the front side of my face. The former sergeant at arms is an FBI informant. Who will be the sergeant at arms now?

It's The Thought That Discounts

The hand is random whether on deck or composed of playing cards, of read or read and weep. The bible study group has commandeered the corner coffee shop so may the celebration of the senses and the flesh commence. Your prophecies align with my attention span. I sleepwalk past the Plain of Jars. Its cornea irregular, the moon is bibbed or bearded and has ears. One can but drive a truck through five of seven founding fathers' private utterances. Bodies on two operating tables, which of you is vacant, which is mine? Third person squared, nine hands on each of ten pianos, half step, half step, Simon says that Simon says that Simon says, The shadows wanting sun are functional once lungs, once lungs are cleared to land.

Free The Aegis!

The faces in the made-up mirror nearer than they seem, the pores pour over, naming poisons, implementing dreams. The one's abundance is the other's lack. The eyes of Texas are the windows of the windows of block walls. The amplitude of oscillation asymptotically approaches zero. As bones will be bones and not just for the nonce, in cubic corners may they wear their pointed hats. As biorhythm gone awry, I'm asking more. The source is not the course. Placebos grow on trees. The source is not the course. Placebos grow on trees.

Hook And Eye

Circumstances everywhere, nor one iota of extenuation. With some rules not yet suspended, I'm proceeding at a fraction of the speed of light and in my polar slumber I rely on strangers' bad intentions as how else would I be toughened up? As with collisions in slow motion so when ice is thinner than existence, what whites won't they take for whites of eyes? I say serenity is earned. In service of the greater good, the words I have a way with will have previously had a way with me — it's only symmetry. I've squared the circle and I know what side my butter's breaded on, my ice cream fried. Each age an age of innocence to the ensuing, endlessly ensuing, may my litigation follow through and hook and eye coordination make of me an athlete. What's the probability that we'll devise an afterlife that we can live with?

Photon

Are you looking for your luminescence where the dark is good or where you found it last time? As one crow sophisticate makes pyramids of quantum possibilities, one innocent collapses laughing. One's not unidentified if one's a flying object and one lets on that the cumulative distribution tends to one. You tell the octopuses of your dream. The octopuses say, Don't dream that way. Take my advice and get a half-life. Don those hour glasses and traverse the corresponding non-self-intersecting path.

Mechanical Advantage

An isolated biorhythm makes a face that's suitable for radio or mother's love, your choice. An ozone of cicadas jealously amends all known agendas. Matched with assets they'll *be* assets and when orbiting a variable access they'll be helices, maybe believers. As my vertical homunculus knows nothing of that horizontal ladder, deep in an interior I'll have the pact to end all pacts. It's vacuum versus vacuum in the presidential residence and back to the unnatural. Ask any object of affection how all objects of affection ought to be addressed and use the proper pronoun please.

Ex Falso Quodlibet

As earth beats air and air beats fire so fire beats water and as Brownian as my emotion when suspended in a biosphere so figments of imagination dancing in the lap of plasma. By tripods of expertise, of twenty of the funniest near-death experiences I would have nineteen. The walking contradiction or the numbered lucky customer, the winner of the shopping spree, I'm asking, why the bifurcation? The taxonomy of non-existence is the family tree.

The Contact Sport

Ten thousand hours et voila the origin of all coordinates, the tabling of motions, your diploma. By their very nature jokes are practical that end in injury. Will you design with me a contact sport that involves tax cuts and deregulation, universal consciousness and quantum dots? You might as well be resurrected in advance of perpetuity. You might as well put your own chest of medals and mild manners on before assisting others. As the a priori's willing but the a posteriori's weak, two faces make no vase. Shall we compute the probability that we'll grow tired of winning?

Watercolor

As if their solvent were not water they would be opaque. Their déjà vu removed, their affect flat, two faces make no vase. The weathers dressed in feathers flock apart. With planets' masses what time-space continuum would they not warp? I'll use to my advantage that the gospels generally agree and that they differ when it suits me. Stripe, meet Spot. It truly is a blessing: from the North pole I can't but go South.

Expected Value

One. As the inner child is remotely controlled the inner child's electric eye is spinning rapidly so if you have suggestions for the inner child don't tap the glass; the inner child's exotic fish will see you shortly. With your rate of change proportional to that of your replacement, you may asymptotically approach the center of the aforementioned spectrum. Panama or camouflaged, your hat is musical or missing and your love that of the uncorrupted.

Two. Seeing red you may at last locate your motive and may reverse engineer one big bang. By their fruits you know their vegetables, their good cops by their bad, their dogs, their cats. You'll be removed but by a trail of crumbs. To call the question or to stave off random thoughts you'll claim all laughter is the same, and then you'll stifle laughter.

Three. Talking dogs are walked into a bar. The silence that of matte black boxes, outs are lights and I'm directing traffic. Good Samaritan am I and voluntary too, communicating as from stem to stern by flag my loyalty to my own mechanism. Blaming matriarchs are marching three by three. Nor linear nor angular, I've no momenta to remember. Only pleasant plants to cultivate, my isotopes are half alive. What mass is not a mass of hats, what plain no plain of jars? Be ye not brains in vats. May only natural nightly doubts arise.

Four. Condemn them mother of interstices, they had their chance. The microscopic flaw will propagate and boys be boys. To laminate is only human, followers to blossom and the google car will take directions from the random traffic cop, not blink an eye. I'm in an aisle and positing an option. Render me seaworthy. Break a rule on my behalf. As some of us are fabricated in God's image more than others some of us are fabricated in God's image more than others.

Five. The magic is in what was meant to happen, levitating bodies on their best behaviors, not a blinding moonshine not distilled. But offering what's left of me to silly science, three delectables in my periphery are evanescing equally as opportunities are lost, as labyrinthine lungs, eternities of burning feathers and the things that happen in the night and in the town of A and not A in the town of A and not A stay.

On Stalking the Apostle Paul

Not every permutation rings a bell. The expectation is not mathematical that calculates itself. Surprise. The wheel is yet to be invented properly, the heart massaged. They say they're timelines but they're not. Lip reading between beehives, more than three axes of symmetry are breached. I'm blinking on and off. The oracle says just what you would think an implicated oracle would say. The aftershock is sought therefore the lilacs last. The dog's velocity the cat's acceleration, mirror neurons interact in atmospheres of planets past. To be an antipode exactly match. The pendula in pockets singing I've got logarithms, the best bulletproofing is the natural act.

Scenic Overlook

Sleep Start

The milk and cookies went untouched and in the center of the level was a bubble was the sun. The father of the light bulb had an elephant electrocuted and a random sample of white men, as white as if they'd seen a ghost, was chosen. They're a people. They're a people and a bubble. They're a people and a bubble and a puddle as all triplets and all twins who witness this agree. There is a dotted line then guiding light then short-term gain. The hand that feeds you is food too.

Scenic Overlook 1

Speak to me through my appreciation, gentle precipice, there's no square inch unpopulated by the beneficiaries of catastrophes and victims of success who for an answer can't take yes. Success as contrapuntal as an evil clone, the follow through is trouble to extrapolation and extrapolation canceled by the right of people to keep and bear arms. The war that I am studying rewrites itself. There are suitcases full of money, faith and credit notwithstanding. In my flesh as yet subtended angles may diminish and peripheries go dark. Compatible with shadow are their cardboard cutouts and their 3D dreams in vain. Last in, first out, an alternate reality, I help the gods that help themselves.

Scenic Overlook 2

The labyrinth is re-imagined and the monolith is made opaque. The oblate spheroid spins until it's dizzy and its stumble funny. My delight is in upending empty cardboard boxes. Words for water everywhere but none convincing to a fish, I put a foot on Satan's Book and swear no other random passenger is looking amorously at me. Now they're predators, now prey. The anvil's quicker than the hammer and the hammer's quicker than the stirrup. Moral compasses abound. Assuming only that the empty set exists, I'm saying, Throw away those old hypotheses and self-propel. An honest asteroid contains no rage.

Scenic Overlook 3

Vitruvian or gingerbread man, count your curses minus one by minus one. If alternately sink and source, if Armageddon's called off maybe later Armageddon's called back on. Peninsulas are peopled. Inlets blend. The heart-shaped box composed of heart-shaped boxes, moral arcs don't know which way they bend. Of shards and garbage, shipping crates say This Side Down. The weather entities are gesturing at green screens, ridiculing clouds. Some lines are lit up. Eyes on stalks are having either all or none of it and voting with their feeling feet. As human nature hates the vacuum so disruption loves the placid pond.

Scenic Overlook 4

Juxtaposing overtones, eliminating middlemen, the coral is pure color. An unstable isotope endears itself and turns the curve of earth so to be saved from the effects of levitation. An existence to come into suddenly and silently, a quantity of mercy notwithstanding and of cylinders the ends identify though oppositely oriented. First Klein bottles conquer nature, then they're millionaires and following the bouncing ball. I'm bent as backwards as I can be. Mirror neuron, friend of Other, who's the least self-serving of us all? As midnight like the north pole is associated via spherical projection with infinity, a point horizon on which no event takes place, accountable infinity is blabbing, taking blame and taking blame. Not with us so against us, shoes for industry and ethical consideration for the clueless, let the ethical distinguish left from right. I do therefore I'm beautiful and let the loser choose.

Scenic Overlook 5

Pursuant to the Doppler Shift the ants are marching three by three, because why not, the geese are in a double V. Before ye eat blaspheme. As cats stand in for dogs and Plato's chair's erroneously represented by a table, so Diogenes be careful what you wish for. I have bad news. Also, I have bad news. He who has no calluses is not a laborer and shot. If three degrees of freedom simplify to two degrees of freedom, on some summer afternoon and in some corner of the room a cricket, there's no turning back. There's no emotion but in figment of imagination and it's meat and right to contemplate the blackened catfish soberly, though sometimes woefully inadequate and sometimes overkill. I'm thinking, Geez Louise, do they know something I don't know?

Scenic Overlook 6

Though I'm unable to absorb it by osmosis, moss is positively plausibly maroon. In flashy camouflage they brandish tiki torches. Alternate realities attach. No matter that it's on the moon, my footprint is protected by an act of congress. So be spiritual My Adviser, be both first and last to call. As on the eve of alteration, to an ear the sea not sleeping, motors turning over and the better angel of the intersection granting rights of way, should jokes be told or told and old the secret service will investigate. The interval with endpoints (a,b) and (c,d) consists of all points (x,y) such that x is between a and c and y is between b and d amen. My hiding place, my personal experience is yours.

Scenic Overlook 7

I'm relatively prime to predators and singing predators to sleep. A house-sized graviton is balanced on a pinnacle and from thin air I'm pulling pillows. In a sea of teeth a detached paddle wheel epitomizes circulation and my girlfriend's mother wants to know if I'm a communist. My girlfriend says dyed-in-the-wool. The horizontal component may take the vertical for granted not for grins. Bernoulli effects equally offending Vs of geese and trees, a code is broken and sufficient to the minute are glad tidings, the glad tidings yes means no and yes means no. When representing finitude reluctantly, when water or air borne, the candle of an absence mothers' moths. To show it's not so bad, the mayor spends a day in jail.

Scenic Overlook 8

Santa Claus and anti Santa Claus are in agreement: after mastering simultaneity, time travel is a snap. Reality is what most matters. Colorado long ago forgave Balloon Boy's parents. Walking upstream, counter to the earth's rotation, every comment thread devolves to Hitler with some would-be influencer's big brain on display. Year Zero is that of the death of god and neither compasses nor crumbs will show the way. Time travel is a snap. As isotopes past half-life we are asymptotically approaching one of many linear accelerators. Mortals, none the wiser, with a pattern and an anthem we deduce the seventh day.

Citations

Versions of some of these poems first appeared in the following journals and anthologies:

"Sleep Start" in *The American Journal of Poetry;* "Expected Value" in *The Babel Tower Notice Board;* "As Transparent As It Gets" in *Cleaver;* "Stringing Clouds Along," "Quid Pro Quo," and "Woke From Coma Speaking French" in *The Collidescope;* "Ex Falso Quodlibet" in *Columbia Journal;* "Reciprocal" in *DM du Jour;* "Piano Drop," "The Garden Of Earthly Delights," and "The Law Of Large Numbers" in *deLuge Journal;* "After Fact," "Two Science Daily Spin-offs," "As Of," and "Who's On First" in *Die Leere Mitte;* "Scenic Overlook 1, 2, 3, and 4" in *The Experiment Will Not Be Bound: An Experimental Anthology of American Writing;* "For Finite Crime" in *Gris-Gris;* "The Lucky Customer" in *I-70 Review;* "Watercolor" in *Jam & Sand;* "Hook And Eye," "Mechanical Advantage," and "Photon" in *Kaleidoscoped;* "In Dog Years" in *Offcourse;* "On Stalking The Apostle Paul" in *Phoebe;* "Retrospective Proprioception" in *Maintenant;* "The Contact Sport" in *Pithead Chapel;* "When Gravitons Amass" in *Ponder Review* and *Proud to Be: Writing By American Warriors, vol. 10;* "When Correlation Is Causation" in *Sunspot;* "Free The Aegis," "In Which I Kick The Tires," "It's The Thought That Discounts," "Optics," and "Syllogism 5" in *Terror House Magazine;* "Return To Sturgis" in *Timber*.

Twelve poems from the third section comprise the micro-chapbook, *Concurrent Birdsong*, which was published by Ghost City Press.

About the Author

In a past century Heikki Huotari was carried by an undertow into the Atlantic Ocean, was on an airplane that landed in a wheat field, grew up on a subsistence farm, attended a one-room school and spent several summers on a forest-fire lookout tower. Drafted into the US Army for cannon fodder in 1968 (next stop, Vietnam), his application for discharge as a conscientious objector was denied (the Baptist chaplain said his faith was too eclectic) so he fasted to collapse, was intravenously force-fed, court-martialed for refusing to eat, then medically discharged. Having after some years acquired a new personality, he earned a PhD in mathematics and pursued a career in teaching and research, was an enthusiastic and nationally ranked master's marathon runner, discovered the totally tubular convex set and explored its use in the study of non-linear statistical inference and the geometry of Banach spaces. He retired from academia in 2012 and undertook to learn to write creatively. He has published poems in 200 or so literary journals, and books and chapbooks, four of which have won prizes. *When Correlation is Causation* is his fifth collection.

www.ingramcontent.com/pod-product-compliance
Lightning Source LLC
Chambersburg PA
CBHW072206100526
44589CB00015B/2390